Let's Throw a Christmas Party!

WITHDRAWN

Rachel Lynette

PowerKiDS
press™

New York

For Bonnie

Published in 2012 by The Rosen Publishing Group, Inc.
29 East 21st Street, New York, NY 10010

First Edition

Editor: Joanne Randolph
Layout Design: Greg Tucker

Photo Credits: Cover (main) Britt Erlanson/Getty Images; cover (inset), pp. 7, 9, 11, 12, 13 (top), 18 Shutterstock.com; pp. 4–5 Sean Justice/Getty Images; p. 6 (top) Comstock/Getty Images; p. 6 (bottom) Hulton Archive/Getty Images; pp. 8, 17 Jupiterimages/Photos.com/Thinkstock; p. 10 iStockphoto/Thinkstock; p. 13 (bottom) SW Productions/Getty Images; p. 16 Steven Errico/Getty Images; p. 19 Inti St. Clair/Getty Images; p. 20 Adrian Dennis/AFP/Getty Images; p. 21 Richard Kolker/Getty Images; p. 22 Hemera/Thinkstock.

Library of Congress Cataloging-in-Publication Data

Lynette, Rachel.
  Let's throw a Christmas party! / by Rachel Lynette. — 1st ed.
    p. cm. — (Holiday parties)
  Includes index.
  ISBN 978-1-4488-2571-4 (library binding) — ISBN 978-1-4488-2731-2 (pbk.) — ISBN 978-1-4488-2732-9 (6-pack)
  1. Christmas decorations—Juvenile literature. 2. Christmas cooking—Juvenile literature. 3. Entertaining—Juvenile literature. 4. Children's parties—Juvenile literature. I. Title.
  TT900.C4L96 2012
  793.2'2--dc22

                            2010031040

Manufactured in the United States of America

CPSIA Compliance Information: Batch #WW11PK: For Further Information contact Rosen Publishing, New York, New York at 1-800-237-9932

Contents

Christmas is a special time of year. Although Christmas Day is **celebrated** on December 25, most people think of Christmas as a season rather than as one day. For many people, the Christmas season begins after Thanksgiving and ends after New Year's Day. During this time, people enjoy special treats like Christmas cookies and candy canes. They sing Christmas

Most people decorate Christmas trees at Christmastime. German settlers brought this tradition to America in the 1800s.

carols, read Christmas stories, **decorate** Christmas trees, and give Christmas gifts to one another.

People often throw Christmas parties during this time. Going to Christmas parties is a lot of fun. It can be even more fun to throw a party of your own!

Christmas became a holiday in AD 320. It celebrates the birth of Jesus. **Christians** believe that Jesus is the Son of God. Many Christmas **traditions** are not Christian, though. Some traditions came from holidays that were celebrated before Jesus's birth. For example, **ancient** Romans celebrated for 12 days in mid-December to honor the god Saturn. They decorated with branches, trees, and candles. They held many feasts and gave each other gifts.

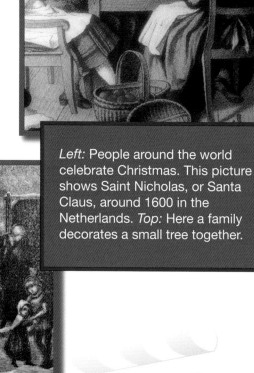

Left: People around the world celebrate Christmas. This picture shows Saint Nicholas, or Santa Claus, around 1600 in the Netherlands. *Top:* Here a family decorates a small tree together.

A Merry Christmas

Other traditions came later. In the 1800s, Christmas caroling and sending Christmas cards became popular in England. Around that same time, people began to decorate Christmas trees in Germany. These traditions spread across Europe and to the Americas.

Many people think of Santa Claus when they think of Christmas.

Santa is not the only one who needs to make lists. If you are going to throw a Christmas party, you need to make them, too! Start by listing all the people you will **invite** to your party. Then you will know how many invitations to send out.

Next you will want to make a list of all the things

You can make invitations by cutting out Christmas shapes, such as snowmen, stockings, or bells, and writing the party information on them. Decorate your invitations with Christmas stickers or glitter.

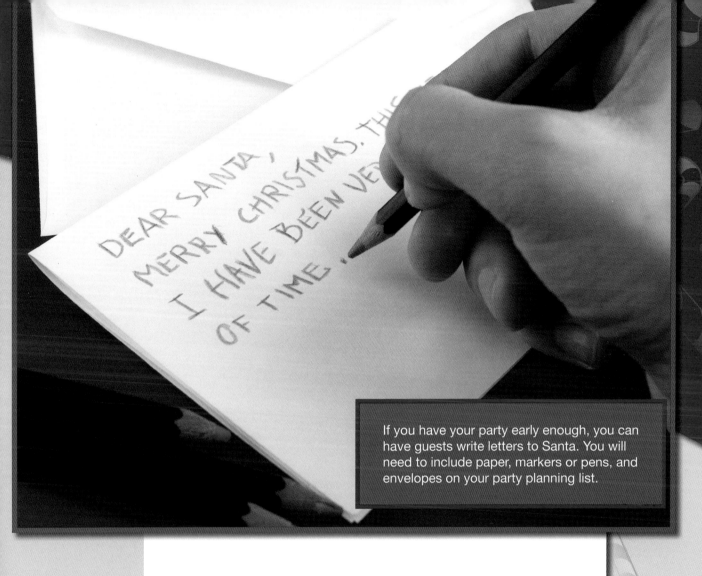

If you have your party early enough, you can have guests write letters to Santa. You will need to include paper, markers or pens, and envelopes on your party planning list.

you will need for your party. Do you want special decorations for the table? What kind of food will you serve? What games would be fun for your guests to play? You may want to ask an adult to help you make your lists.

Set a Merry Table

Red and green are the most traditional Christmas colors. White, blue, gold, and silver will also help make your table bright and fun, though. You can buy paper tablecloths, plates, cups, and napkins in the colors you pick. You can make napkin rings just by using red or green ribbon to tie bows around your napkins.

Red, white, and green table settings and napkins are a good pick for Christmas. Wrap tiny presents to put on each place setting for an extra nice touch!

Use red construction paper to make place cards in the shape of stockings. Glue white cotton balls to the top of each for trim. Write each guest's name on the foot of the stocking. Then untwist paper clips to make hooks. Glue them to the backs of the stockings and hang the stockings from the cups!

Hanging stockings by the fireplace has been a Christmas tradition for hundreds of years. When children wake up in the morning the stockings have been filled with fruit or small gifts.

Christmas Treats and Sweets

What will you serve your guests to eat? How about cheesy candy-cane breadsticks? Knead grated cheddar cheese into bread dough. Then roll the dough into candy cane shapes and bake!

Your guests will also enjoy Christmas cookies. You can use Christmas cookie cutters to make fun Christmas shapes, such

Gingerbread men and gumdrops are yummy Christmas treats. For extra fun, you can serve gingerbread cookies plain and let your guests decorate their own!

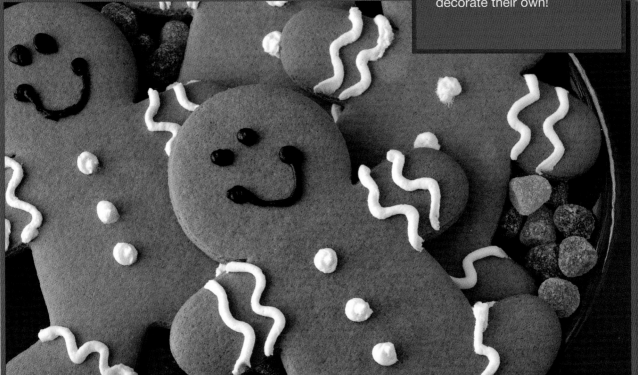

Try giving your guests reindeer cocoa to drink. Give each guest a paper cup with 2 tablespoons of instant cocoa, about 10 mini marshmallows, 3 unwrapped chocolate kisses, and 1 candy cane. Ask an adult to pour hot water into everyone's cup. Your guests can use their candy canes to stir the cocoa!

as stockings, stars, bells, and gingerbread men. Decorate your cookies with green and red frosting, small candies, and sprinkles. For extra fun, you may even want to let your guests decorate their own cookies.

Here is something fun you can do with broken candy canes. Break them into very small pieces and then add them to fudge to make peppermint fudge!

Sheet cakes are a quick and easy food to make for any party. To make yours fit for Christmas, just frost it and sprinkle it with red and green sugar.

Make a Puzzle-Piece Wreath

Your guests will enjoy making Christmas ornaments that they can take home.

What you need:

Old puzzle pieces
Green paint
Glitter
Stickers
Small paper plate
Red construction paper
Scissors
Glue
Red or green ribbon or yarn

What you do:

1

To make a puzzle-piece **ornament**, paint some old puzzle pieces green. Let them dry.

2

Use scissors to cut out the center part of a small paper plate to make a ring. Ask an adult for help if you need it. Paint the ring green and let it dry.

3

Glue the green puzzle pieces all around the ring.

4

Decorate your wreath with glitter and stickers if you like.

5

Cut a bow from red construction paper and glue it on your wreath.

6

Tie a piece of red or green yarn to the top and hang your wreath on your tree.

It is fun to decorate a Christmas tree. You can have decorations ready for your guests to hang on your tree. Your guests may also want to make their own decorations.

One traditional decoration that is fun to make is a popcorn and cranberry garland. To make a garland, each guest will need a long piece of waxed dental

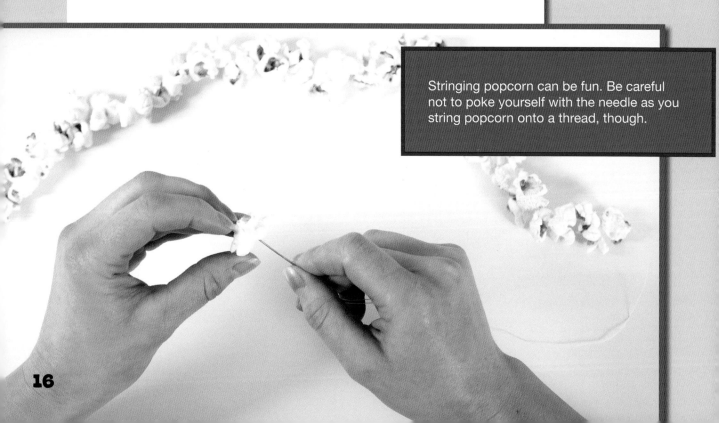

Stringing popcorn can be fun. Be careful not to poke yourself with the needle as you string popcorn onto a thread, though.

These girls have made a paper chain for their tree. Now they are working on stringing some popcorn for a garland. Even young guests can try this activity.

floss and a sewing needle. Thread the needle on the dental floss and tie a knot at the bottom. Then have your guests make chains by pushing the needle and thread through popped popcorn and fresh cranberries. You can tie several chains together to make a really long garland!

Time for Games

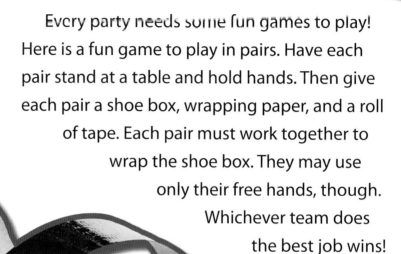

Every party needs some fun games to play! Here is a fun game to play in pairs. Have each pair stand at a table and hold hands. Then give each pair a shoe box, wrapping paper, and a roll of tape. Each pair must work together to wrap the shoe box. They may use only their free hands, though. Whichever team does the best job wins!

For the ribbon-hunt game, cut all the ribbons before the day of your party. You can use ribbons of any color, not just red and green ones.

You may want to give small prizes to the winners of the games. Some good prizes are Christmas stickers, candy canes, a jingle bell necklace, or Christmas socks.

Your guests will also enjoy going on a ribbon hunt. Before your guests arrive, hide pieces of red and green ribbon. The pieces should be different lengths. Your guests must search for the ribbons and tie the ones they find together. The guest with the longest ribbon wins!

The Sugar Plum Fairy Game

Have you ever heard of the Sugar Plum Fairy? She is a character in a **ballet** called *The Nutcracker* that is performed at Christmastime. The ballet is about a young girl named Clara who receives a nutcracker doll as a gift from her uncle.

During *The Nutcracker*, Clara magically gets smaller, and the Nutcracker becomes real. They go to a magical land. There they meet the Sugar Plum Fairy, who is dancing here.

Musical chairs is a fun game for any party. Be sure to have a stereo ready. Give someone who will not be playing the job of starting and stopping the music.

You can play musical chairs using music from *The Nutcracker*! Put chairs in a circle. Make sure you have one fewer chair than the number of people playing. Put on the music. Then have your guests walk or dance around the circle. When the music stops, everyone must take a seat. The person who cannot find a seat is out. The last person left is the Sugar Plum Fairy!

A Time for Giving

It is fun to go to a Christmas party, but it is also important to remember that Christmas is a time for helping other people. One way you can help people in need is to have your guests each bring something to give to **charity**. They could bring canned food to **donate**

Have everyone bring a wrapped present for charity. Christmas is really about giving to others!

to a nearby **food bank**. They could bring warm clothing, blankets, or toys for children who live in homeless shelters.

You might want to ask an adult friend to help you pick a charity and bring the donations there. Giving to others will make you and your guests feel good. That would be a party worth remembering!

Glossary

ancient (AYN-shent) Very old, from a long time ago.

ballet (BA-lay) A type of dance that uses beautiful movements and often tells a story.

celebrated (SEH-luh-brayt-ed) Honored an important moment by doing special things.

charity (CHER-uh-tee) A group that gives help to the needy.

Christians (KRIS-chunz) People who follow the teachings of Jesus Christ and the Bible.

decorate (DEH-kuh-rayt) To add objects that make something prettier or more interesting.

donate (DOH-nayt) To give something away.

food bank (FOOD BANK) A place where food is given to people in need.

invite (in-VYT) To ask people if they will come to a party.

ornament (OR-nuh-ment) A decoration.

traditions (truh-DIH-shunz) Ways of doing things that have been passed down over time.

Index

Web Sites

Due to the changing nature of Internet links, PowerKids Press has developed an online list of Web sites related to the subject of this book. This site is updated regularly. Please use this link to access the list:
www.powerkidslinks.com/hp/xmas/